Lemurs

Lemurs

ON LOCATION

KATHY DARLING

PHOTOGRAPHS BY TARA DARLING

LOTHROP, LEE & SHEPARD BOOKS • MORROW
NEW YORK

ACKNOWLEDGMENTS

We would like to thank Dr. Patricia C. Wright, Professor of Anthropology, State University of New York at Stony Brook, for reading this manuscript for factual accuracy.

A special thank-you to the de Heaulme family, who have protected the lemurs and all the other animals on their land since 1936. Without them, there would be no Berenty Forest.

Thanks also to Dr. Ian Tattersall, at the American Museum of Natural History; Dr. Helen Crowley, the manager of the Berenty Reserve; Dr. Alison Jolly, of Princeton University; Dr. Richard Sussman; and Dr. Russell Mittermeier and the scientists of the Duke Primate Center, for sharing their firsthand knowledge of lemurs with me.

Text copyright © 1998 by Mary Kathleen Darling
Photographs copyright © 1998 by Tara Darling

Library of Congress Cataloging-in-Publication Data
Darling, Kathy. Lemurs on location/Kathy Darling; photographs by Tara Darling.   p. cm.   Includes index.
Summary: Describes the physical characteristics and behavior of different kinds of lemurs encountered on a trip to a forest in southeastern Madagascar.
ISBN 0-688-12539-5 (trade)—ISBN 0-688-12540-9 (library) 1. Lemurs—Juvenile literature. 2. Lemurs—Madagascar—Juvenile literature. [1. Lemurs.] I. Darling, Tara, ill. II. Title. QL737.P95D37 1998
599.8'3—dc21 97-36250 CIP AC

Contents

This ringtail's spine-tingling howl is meant to scare other animals out of its territory.

The Haunted Forest

Oooo-oo-oo! An eerie shriek echoed among the trees. From deep in the woods came hoots and howls, moans, groans, and every other scary sound you've ever heard. It was broad daylight, but as soon as my daughter, Tara, and I stepped into the forest, ghostly forms with glowing eyes appeared in the trees.

The "ghosts" leaped toward us, bouncing from one tree trunk to another. We were trapped by a ring of spooky creatures, all growling and screaming. Tara and I weren't afraid, though. We knew the noisy "ghosts" were really monkeylike animals called lemurs.

With their wide-eyed stares and deafening chorus, the lemurs were trying to frighten us off. Although the display, called "mobbing," is mostly bluff, lemurs are often successful at "singing their troubles away."

Lemur cries are so scary that the first Europeans who heard them believed the forests were haunted. They thought the howling animals were the ghosts of dead people who meant them harm, and called them lemurs. If you don't like your name, just be glad you're not a lemur! Lemur means "spirit of the evil dead."

Lemur-haunted forests are found in Madagascar, a tropical island off the southeast coast of Africa. The fourth largest island on earth, it stretches about three hundred fifty miles from east to west and one thousand miles from north to south. A map of it resembles a giant left footprint with an exceptionally long big toe.

Millions of years ago Madagascar was

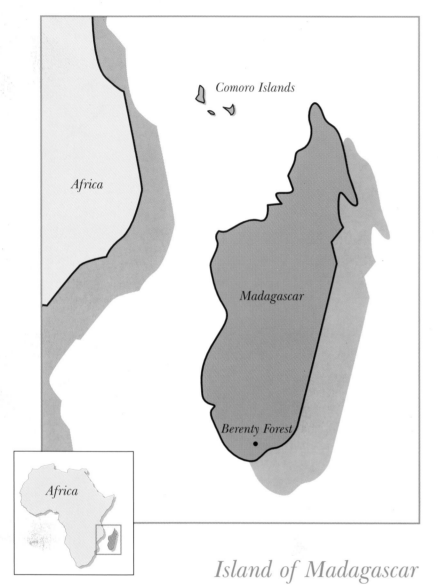

Comoro Islands

Africa

Madagascar

Berenty Forest

Africa

Island of Madagascar

part of Africa. But during one of the big rearrangements of the earth's land masses, Madagascar broke off and moved two hundred fifty miles into the Indian Ocean. The plants and animals on the island evolved in isolation. More than 80 percent of the living things on this minicontinent aren't found anywhere else. They look strange and familiar at the same time.

Lemurs are one of the most puzzling creatures. At first glance they look a lot like monkeys, but on closer examination you are not so sure. Most lemurs have an un-monkeylike face—long like a dog's or a fox's, with whiskers and a wet nose.

The first impression is the right one, though. Lemurs are our relatives. They're primates, members of the same group of mammals that includes monkeys, apes, and us. Lemurs and the other primates that rely on smell rather than sight—bush babies, lorises, pottos, and tarsiers—are called prosimians. These small-brained primates are thought to resemble our own ancestors.

Tara and I went to a small forest called

The lemurs of Berenty Forest are "habituated." They are wild but used to having humans around them. This troop of ringtails wants Kathy to give them banana snacks.

Berenty in southeast Madagascar to study lemurs. Berenty is a great place to watch them. In this private reserve, owned and protected by the de Heaulme family, scientists have observed lemurs for years, and the animals there are no longer afraid of people; they are "habituated."

Most lemurs are nocturnal, but three of Berenty's most interesting lemurs are diurnal, which means they are active during the day. Tara's favorites were the big white lemurs called sifakas. She loved the way they bounced from tree to tree in great leaps and danced a graceful ballet on the ground.

I liked the troops of quarrelsome ring-tailed lemurs best. Mischievous and playful, they were great fun to watch—although sometimes I think they were having as much fun watching us.

The most common of the diurnal lemurs in Madagascar are the gentle browns. All lemurs are smelly, but the browns have a particularly strong body odor that makes them hard to choose as a favorite.

The first thing we learned was that

You could never win a staring contest with a sifaka. Lemurs don't blink. They have a nictitating membrane, or third eyelid, that sweeps across the eyeball to moisten it.

The brown lemur on the left can be identified as a female by the black fur that forms a cap on her head. A red-orange cap identifies the brown lemur on the right as a male.

sifakas, the largest of the Berenty lemurs, are definitely the bosses of the forest. And it didn't take us long to discover that ringtails are dominant over browns. Although ringtails and browns are about the same size, the ringtails travel in larger groups and are more aggressive.

Lemur watchers like us have a hard time telling males and females apart, at least in some species. Male and female sifakas look alike. So do male and female ringtails. They are the same size and color. Both male and female browns are chestnut brown with a darker tail, a black face, clown eyebrows, and an orange beard. But the sexes have different fur patterns. Males have a little orange cap, and females have a black or gray cap.

One of the most exciting things about lemur study is knowing how much there is to learn. With new species of lemurs being found and some known species never having been studied, there is a lot of work and years of great discoveries ahead for young scientists willing to go where no one has ever gone before.

Leapin' 2 Lemurs

Trees are the key to understanding primates and why we are the way we are. The history of the primate family began in the trees and continued there as it branched out into more than two hundred species. Even today only human primates have really left the trees.

Frogs, squirrels, and lots of other animals live in trees too. So primates obviously have some other things in common. Exactly what credentials are necessary for membership in the primate family?

A pair of seemingly insignificant features has allowed primates to take to the trees—a hand with movable fingers that gives them the ability to climb by grasping, and a pair of forward-facing eyes. With eyes in the front of the face, it is possible to judge distances accurately. That's a big advantage for an animal that leaps from branch to branch.

Every lemur can leap, but the long-legged sifakas are the world's champions. No other animal, not even a kangaroo, can outjump the acrobatic members of the Indri family of lemurs from a standstill. The nine-pound sifaka could spring up and sit on a ten-foot-high basketball hoop. (Michael Jordan, eat your heart out!) But the sifakas' broad-jumping ability is what really dazzles. Indri lemurs can easily cover more than thirty feet in a single leap from one tree trunk to another.

However, sifakas cheat—just a little. They've got a broad fur-covered flap of skin running along each side of their body from armpit to wrist. By holding out their arms

A ringtail lemur uses all of its jumping ability when leaping among these spiny sisal plants, which are grown to make rope at Berenty.

The sifakas' hands and feet were designed for grasping branches. The fingers move only as a group, and the thumb and fingers operate like a clamp.

and spreading the flaps, sifakas can increase the length of a jump by gliding.

To be a good jumper, an animal has to be especially designed for it, and lemurs are. How far an animal can jump is determined by takeoff speed. And, surprisingly, takeoff speed does not directly depend on a creature's size or weight. In mammals jumping ability is based on muscle power. There are no secret superstrong muscles in the hind legs of the leaping lemurs. It's ordinary muscle, just like yours and mine. Lemurs just have a lot more of it in relation to their body weight. The skinny sifaka may not look like a body builder, but it's got twice as much muscle power as any human.

All the power in a lemur's leap comes from its long hind legs. When it wants to jump, a sifaka lets go with its arms and twists its body around to select a landing site. Then, pushing off with its feet, the lemur launches itself into the air in an upright position. With arms extended and tail trailing for balance, the leaper always makes a feet-first landing. Legs then fold into a crouch to soften the impact. Well-padded fingers and toes also absorb some of the shock.

The palms of lemur hands and the soles of their feet are rough and leathery. The thick skin is very tough. It has to be. Some of the trees lemurs leap around in have three-inch-long thorns. How they manage to do it without injuring themselves is a mystery.

Sifakas also know how to get the most from their muscles. At rest they hang on to a tree with their arms and legs folded and their body pressed close to the trunk. This tree-hugging position, which keeps the animal's center of gravity close to the trunk, requires the least amount of effort to hold on. The bent joints also provide a mechanical advantage when the lemur jumps. Ankles, knees, and hips straighten in a leap, like a series of extending levers, and boost the power.

The leaping lemurs have another trick. It's an energy-saving series of rapid leaps called ricochets. The ricochet's energy conservation system works much like that of a bouncing ball. A ball can bounce many times because whenever it hits the ground, energy is transferred to the rubber, stored there, and then recycled into another bounce. Lemurs gather some of the energy from each jump in their tendons—elastic structures that join muscle to bone—and use that stored energy for the next jump.

In order to have space to ricochet, the sifakas travel through a forest about five feet above the ground, staying on the parts of the trunks that are well below the leafy branches. Ringtails, browns, and other

This is no ballerina. Male sifakas have a scent gland on their throats. Often you can see a dark stain around it, like the one on this dancer's neck.

species that don't ricochet travel higher in the canopy.

Leaping is easy for lemurs. On the other hand, walking is difficult. Ringtail and brown lemurs move along on the ground with their rear ends stuck up in the air. The sifakas' hind legs are so long that they cannot walk on four feet at all. Sifakas have just about the same body proportions as humans. However, unlike us, they are built to use both legs at once. So on the ground they hop—with both feet together in a sideways dance that looks like a comical ballet. With each spring the sifaka waves its arms up and down, alternating between chest and head height. Strange as it looks, it's a good way to travel. The lemur ballerinas cover ten feet with each bound.

Mother lemurs leap for two. Babies are carried wherever Mom goes. A newborn, just three inches long including the tail, must be strong enough to cling onto its mother's fur as soon as it is born. The mother needs her hands for leaping and cannot hold her baby.

For the first few days a baby clings to the underside of its mother's belly. If it rode on her back, a hawk or a buzzard could snatch it off while Mom was eating in the treetops. In a few days the little lemur wraps its body around Mom's waist, like a belt. After several weeks the baby changes positions for a seat with a view, riding on Mom's back like a little jockey. At two months the young rider is ready to play a lemur game called "leave mother and dash back." When the baby is five or six months old, the free rides are cut off. The reason is plain to see: Babies hold on by grabbing a handful of fur, and the moms have bare patches where their fur has been pulled out by heavy hitchhikers.

From October to May Berenty is very hot. At midday the lemurs all seek out shady branches and take naps. As you might imagine, sleeping on a branch is not without danger. Snoozing lemurs sometimes lose their balance, and nap time ends with a crash!

Napping lemurs often form what Tara and I called a "locomotive line." One animal grabs a tree trunk and others snuggle up

The arms and tail are used for balance when the sifaka must travel on the ground.

with their big jumping legs enclosing the lemur in front. To us, this looked just like the train games we played as children. We thought ringtails made the best locomotives because they added sound effects. The whole row purred like cats.

When it is dark, lemurs sleep high in the canopy. But during the day, they snooze on shady branches closer to the ground. The sifakas like to nap in V-shaped branches with their hands resting on their knees and their tails curled up like watch springs. On the hottest days we saw ringtails drape themselves over a branch with arms and legs dangling down. The long black-and-white-striped tails look like giant caterpillars on the branches. We could always find out where brown lemurs were napping by listening. Restless nappers grunted to one another, and it sounded something like snoring.

No more free rides! The bald spot where this baby brown lemur has pulled out the fur on his mother's back is a sign that he is getting too big for her to carry.

This sifaka family is settling into a "locomotive line" for a midday snooze. The curled-up tail is a common sleeping position.

Every time Tara and I saw the ringtails running with their black-and-white tails sticking straight in the air like this, we thought of the Cat in the Hat. Ringtails spend more time on the ground than do any other lemurs.

The Big Stink Fight

The ringtail troop was on the move when we spotted them. Twenty-five strong, they swaggered down the wide path that marked the edge of their territory. Up front, in charge of the border patrol, were the adult females. The biggest males followed close behind. Then, in the most protected spots, came the mothers with young babies. And, at the end of the raggedy column, were the young males—pushing, shoving, and squabbling among themselves as usual. Everyone was on the lookout for members of the neighboring troop of ringtails. This was disputed territory.

Every few yards one or another of the troop paused at a smooth-barked tree to put a fresh scent mark on the boundary line. An old female scampered up to a spot where there were many old markings. She put both hands on the ground and lifted her rear as high as possible on the trunk and rubbed scent from a gland near the base of her tail onto the bark. Within a minute, another female deposited her body scent there too. The urge to mark territory was overwhelming. Soon there was a line of both males and females waiting for a turn at the tree trunk.

Males hogged the marking place because they needed time to make two kinds of markings. After marking the trunk with an acrobatic handstand, a male would grab a twig in both hands. Sharp, bony spurs on each wrist dug into the bark, clicking loudly as they made deep scratches filled with scent from glands on the ringtail's forearms.

A ringtail marks his territory with scent from glands in his forearms.

Suddenly the screaming members of a rival troop erupted from the trees on the other side of the path. The females rushed to protect their territory. Charging at the attacking females, they made short, loud calls like a small dog's bark. Sharp teeth drew

blood and grabbing fingers sent fur flying in the opening action.

Where were the males? Hopping, skipping, squealing, yawning, and excitedly marking saplings in the background until finally they got up enough courage to challenge the rival troop's males. Ringtail females do battle with tooth and claw. The males stink fight!

To prepare for the smelly battle, one of the young males sat in the leaf litter and pulled his black-and-white ringed tail between his legs. Drawing it over the glands on his forearms, he loaded it with scent. Then, squealing and pinning back his ears, the stink fighter advanced on all fours toward another male. His scent-loaded tail arched over his back and he beat it up and down, fanning gusts of his "weapon" at the opposition. At ten feet the waving tail caused the "stunk up" lemur to draw back in obvious disgust. I was just as close, but I couldn't smell a thing. The scent that is so repulsive to lemurs is nearly odorless to humans.

Only male ringtails stink fight, but all

lemurs use scent to communicate. Monkeys, apes, and humans get most of their information visually. Prosimians can see well, and in color too, but the largest part of their brain is devoted to processing information about smells. Almost all lemurs have long snouts. This kind of face doesn't have the muscles needed to produce the expressions that other primates use to show their feelings. Prosimians communicate with a variety of smells instead. To produce the scents, lemurs have glands in various places on their body and a special organ on the roof of their mouth to detect the chemicals released by the scent glands. Scent contains messages about territory boundaries, a willingness to breed, and family membership.

Whether it is day or night, you know when brown lemurs are near. They have a very strong smell and quite generously rub it all over one another and the places they like. It is a good thing for us lemur watchers that the brown lemurs don't stink fight. Humans can definitely smell their scent, and believe me, it is not a pleasant experience.

The strong smell does not mean brown lemurs are dirty. In fact, they spend hours each day on personal hygiene, as do all lemurs. Grooming is a pleasurable group activity and helps to form bonds between individual animals. To avoid bad hair days,

The winner! Armed only with a stench, this young "stink fighter" defeated his opponent from ten feet away. Some researchers say they can detect a ringtail's fighting odor, but Tara and I couldn't smell a thing.

lemurs tidy up their velvety coats with their teeth and claws, not their fingers. The lemur family has flat nails on all digits except the second toe on each foot. This toe has a grooming claw that sticks up at a sharp angle. It's great for scratching and comes in handy for cleaning ears.

On all lemur species except the aye-aye, the six lower front teeth stick straight out and are used to pull out fur mats, untangle hair, and remove foreign objects. These grooming teeth, called a tooth comb, are kept clean with a built-in toothbrush. Under the tongue there is a fringed structure with sharpened and hardened points that can be pushed forward to clean fur out of the front teeth.

In ringtail troops, it's females who get beauty treatments. Males are always offering to groom them. The troops have no real leader, but the females are definitely in charge. They are the warrior princesses, the front line in an attack and the first in defense when the troop is threatened. A ringtail troop is a sisterhood. A female baby will remain with her birth family all her life, but males leave the troop when they mature.

Females claim the best bits of food and the choicest sleeping spots. They are the same size as the males and show no fear of them. New mothers are especially short-tempered with males. When one approaches a baby, the mother will raise a warning hand. If the offending male doesn't back off, he usually loses a tuft of fur for his curiosity.

Ringtailed lemurs are very quarrelsome creatures, and not all the fights are as harmless as stink fights. Jump fights are serious battles with biting and scratching. Most are between males for the right to breed with a female. Thankfully the breeding season is very short—less than a week for the entire troop, with each female being receptive for only a single day. Male aggression is so dangerous during breeding season that, if continued over several months instead of a single week in April, it could result in the males killing each other off. Even so, most

All lemurs like to be groomed, even the quick-tempered ringtails.

It's a good thing that mating season for ringtails lasts only a single week in April. Jump fights over females can be deadly and leave few males unscarred.

older male ringtails have big black scars in their velvety gray fur as the result of these violent jump fights.

In spite of the ringtails' ill-tempered behavior, the constant bickering and cuffing, they spend a lot of time in contact with one another. Grooming sessions take up most of their free time. And on winter afternoons they form snooze huddles: a big ball of snuggling lemurs with tails and feet sticking out in all directions.

Unlike the rowdy ringtails, the shy sifakas live in small family groups. Shy doesn't mean serious, though. Sifakas are full of fun. Even the adults join in energetic games. Midday, when the troop leaves the hot, sunny canopy for the shade below, is the time for playing. Tara and I loved watching sifaka acrobatics. There was always a game of tag or leapfrog with somersaults at the end. Funniest, though, were the wrestling contests. In these slow-motion duels, the sifakas dangled from an arm or a leg and battled it out using the other three limbs. They always made us laugh.

Brown lemurs are less playful than their ringtail and sifaka relatives. Although they travel in groups, the groups change constantly in size and membership. Above all else, browns are adaptable. That's probably why they are the most numerous of all the big lemurs.

This adult sifaka was just settling into the crook of a tree for a nap, but the frisky youngster had other ideas. Luckily for him, even adult sifakas enjoy a good wrestling match.

Eat Your Vegetables, Please

The reason a lemur's life is tied to the trees is because that's where the food is. Sifakas, ringtails, and browns can live in the same territory because they eat different parts of the same trees. The ringtails are fruit lovers, browns favor flowers and buds, and the sifakas prefer a diet of leaves.

What's for dinner depends on the season, if you're a ringtailed lemur. If fruit is available, ringtails will eat that first. Kily fruits are their favorite. Other items on the menu are flowers, seeds, and tender new plants. Leaves are a final choice.

In tropical Madagascar, where the trees are always green, some lemurs have become leaf-eating specialists. The sifakas have a very long intestine that contains bacteria to help digest a tough, leafy diet. All year long

the white lemurs happily munch greenery, even some that is known to contain powerful doses of toxic substances. One of the trees in Berenty has seeds that make ringtail and brown lemurs vomit, but the sifakas consume large quantities with no problem. Because sifakas get all the water they need from the plants they eat, they can also live in the deserts of Madagascar. Although sifakas have never been seen drinking, we watched them lick the morning dew from their hair in the hot summer months.

Unlike the sifakas, ringtails and browns need water every day. They drink from tree hollows, the leaves of plants, and puddles on the ground. Although they are careful to keep away from each other in the trees, ringtails and browns often meet near puddles

Lemurs visit each part of their range every week to ten days, so damage to food plants is spread evenly over the entire area.

Lemurs like this ringtail can breathe and swallow at the same time. We humans can't.

when water is scarce. Browns, even if there are more of them, usually run away from the always-ready-to-start-something ringtails.

When lemurs come down from the trees to eat or drink, they take turns standing guard. Protecting the troop is serious business, and the lookouts don't even nibble on a blade of grass till they are off duty.

Brown lemurs have a more varied diet than most lemurs. They'll eat fruit and flowers when they can find them and leaves when they can't. But the brown's favorite treats are tree saps and gums. Anchoring their sharp canines in the bark, they scrape the tree trunk with their tooth combs and collect the sweet goo. In times of drought, browns have been seen eating such un-lemurlike foods as cockroaches, caterpillars, spiders, gecko lizards, chameleons, and birds' eggs. But the main part of all diurnal lemurs' meals is vegetable. Leaves and grasses are not very high in calories, so the lemurs have to eat a lot of them. In fact, most of their time is spent eating. Lemurs can stuff in food and drink faster than any human because, unlike us, they can breathe and swallow at the same time.

It is easy to get separated from your family when you are busy eating in a dense forest. So the lemurs make little contact calls when they can't see one another.

Each species of lemur has a vocabulary. There's a contact call, a sound that means danger from above (usually a hawk), and several different ones that identify dangers on the ground.

"Coo-coo" means "I'm here. Where are you?" to a sifaka. If sifakas are lost, they loudly repeat "sifaka." This sound, which they make when they are worried about something, became their name.

Ringtails don't coo. They mew, much like a cat, to keep in touch. That's how they got their scientific name of *Lemur catta*.

Brown lemurs make a piglike grunt as a locator call. They grunt to keep in contact, as a greeting, and also to show curiosity. But when a brown wants to draw attention to a possible source of danger, it makes a gagging sound.

Brown lemurs love gooey lumps of tree gum. The tasty treat takes a lot of chewing, though.

When the browns, ringtails, and sifakas are asleep at night, another lemur comes out to eat in the forest of Berenty. Lepilemurs like this mother and baby are strictly tree dwellers. They have never been seen on the ground.

An Island 5 *Out of Time*

It is easy to see that the monkeylike ringtail, sifaka, and brown lemurs are members of our own primate family. Identifying some of the other lemurs as our close relatives is a bit harder. The smallest lemurs resemble mice. Many of the middle-sized species seem to be more closely related to squirrels.

In all there are about thirty different kinds of lemurs. Scientists say "about" thirty because they aren't sure of the exact number yet. With new methods of examining DNA, animals once thought to be subspecies have been reclassified as separate species, and lemurs previously unknown to science have been discovered on recent expeditions. Besides, so much of Madagascar's remaining forest is unexplored that it is highly likely that there are still species left to discover.

Millions of years ago the lemur family was a lot larger. Lemurs ranged over every continent except Antarctica. Fossils of more than a hundred species have been found, including one, larger than a gorilla, that climbed through the trees of prehistoric Madagascar. All of the monster lemurs are extinct. The largest living species weighs a mere fifteen pounds. Unlike the disappearance of the dinosaurs, the extinction of the giant lemurs is no mystery to scientists. They know what happened. Monkeys and apes and man happened!

The smaller-brained lemur ancestors couldn't compete with their smarter, more aggressive cousins, and they died out almost everywhere. The group of ancestral lemurs that lived on Madagascar was lucky, though.

The island broke off from the African mainland and drifted out into the Indian Ocean before humans, apes, or even monkeys evolved. There were no large predators on the island—until humans found their way there about fifteen hundred years ago. Once humans arrived, the trouble started. They gobbled up all the ten-foot-tall aepyornis, the largest birds that ever lived. They feasted on giant tortoises till there were none left. And they devoured the fifteen largest species of lemur. About three hundred fifty years ago, when the first natural history books were written about the island originally called Lemuria, all the big species were gone.

The first people to see lemurs thought they were ghosts. That is what they may become if something isn't done to stop the destruction of Madagascar's forests. Chopped down, bulldozed, turned into rice fields— these forests are disappearing faster than those of the Amazon or Africa. More than 85 percent of them are already gone. And if the forests disappear, so will the lemurs. The

The adaptable browns are the most numerous of the day-active lemurs, but even they are threatened by the disappearance of Madagascar's forests. All the lemurs are now on the Endangered Species List.

situation is so desperate that it has been necessary to put all the lemur species on the Endangered Species List to help protect them.

Saving the forests and the lemurs is a race against time. Many people are trying to help. Americans at Duke University have set up a captive breeding program in North Carolina to safeguard the most endangered lemurs. Duke's scientists are keeping lemurs in their zoo in case conservation efforts are not successful. But Duke University and other organizations, including the World Wildlife Fund and the United Nations, are also working with the Malagasy government and concerned people, like the de Heaulme family, to save the remaining forests. Their goal is generation after generation of lemurs living wild and free.

Long ago, when people first came to Madagascar and saw lemurs posed like this ringtail, they thought the lemurs were praying to the sun. Today scientists believe that they are sunbathing to warm up after a cool night.

Lemur Facts

(pronounced LEE-muhr)

Names: Ringtailed lemur: scientific name *Lemur catta*, Malagasy name maki. Brown lemur: scientific name *Eulemur fulvus*, Malagasy names gidro, varika. Sifaka: scientific name *Propithecus verreauxi*, Malagasy name sifaka.

Number of species: Species number varies from 32 to 50 as the result of differing methods of classification. Additional undescribed species may exist.

Size: Males and females are about the same size in all lemur species. Smallest: mouse lemur, 1 ounce. Largest: Indri, 15 pounds. Ringtail: weight 7–8 1/2 pounds, body length 12–17 inches, tail 20–24 inches. Brown: weight 7–9 pounds, length 12–18 inches, tail 18 inches. Sifaka: weight 9 pounds, length 15–20 inches, tail 18–24 inches.

Life expectancy: Ringtails, browns, and sifakas all live between 20 and 30 years.

Food: Mostly vegetation, including grasses, leaves, fruits, flowers, seeds, and saps. The diet of some species is restricted to a single type of plant, such as bamboo. In times of drought the diet may be expanded to include insects, spiders, small lizards, eggs, and fungi. The smaller lemurs eat insects and invertebrates regularly.

Social organization/behavior: Nocturnal species are usually solitary. Diurnal ones form pair bonds or troops. Females are dominant in almost all lemur species.

Color: Brown, gray, red, white, or black—usually in patterns. In most species males and females are marked alike. Eyes can be startling yellow, brilliant orange, Day-Glo green, or bright blue.

Reproduction: All species have live babies. Single births are the norm. Gestation: Ringtails, 132 days. Browns, 120 days. Sifakas, 162 days.

Population: All lemurs are on the Endangered Species List. Exact numbers are unknown for each species. Browns are the most widespread and are thought to be the most numerous of the large species. Others, such as the golden-crowned sifaka and the golden bamboo lemur, probably number only a few hundred.

Range/habitat: Lemurs live only on Madagascar and the neighboring Comoro Islands. They are found in all ecosystems, ranging from rain forest to spiny desert.

Index

(Entries in *italics* refer to photos and captions.)